THE PAIN OF CHRIST
AND THE SORROW OF GOD

Gerald Vann, O.P.

THE PAIN OF CHRIST *AND THE* SORROW OF GOD

Lenten Meditations

SOPHIA INSTITUTE PRESS
Manchester, New Hampshire

Nihil obstat: Ricardus Roche, S.T.D., Censor Deputatus

Imprimatur: Joseph, Archiepiscopus Birmingamiensis

Birmingham, November 4, 1947

Approbatio Ordinis:

Nihil obstat: Fr. Gualterus Gumbley, O.P., F.R.HIST.S.

Imprimi potest: Fr. Hilarius J. Carpenter, O.P., Prior Provincialis Angliae

London, November 17, 1947

Sophia Institute Press
Box 5284, Manchester, NH 03108
1-800-888-9344

www.SophiaInstitute.com

Sophia Institute Press® is a registered trademark of Sophia Institute.

paperback ISBN 978-1-64413-479-5

ebook ISBN 978-1-64413-480-1

Library of Congress Control Number: 2020950959

First printing

Contents

Preface

The first six of the following chapters represent the substance of a Lenten course of sermons preached at Westminster Cathedral in 1947. In these sermons, some of the aspects of the problem of pain were touched upon, but inevitably many loose ends had to be left; and therefore a further chapter, *The Sorrow of God*—first printed separately as an Aquinas Paper but now out of print—has been added in the hope of supplementing and elucidating some of the points raised.

—G.V.

THE PAIN OF CHRIST
AND THE SORROW OF GOD

1

THE AGONY IN THE GARDEN

So Jesus came, and they with him, to
a plot of land called Gethsemani.

—Matthew 26:36, Knox

The history of mankind is a love story. It is the story of how man was made for God and then became estranged from God, but in the end, after many struggles and many sorrows, is to come back again to God, to be happy again in the end.

And the climax of that story begins in a garden, in Geth-semani; because it is there that begin those events we call the Passion of our Lord, the events that make it possible for us, here and now, to find our way home to God. And so those events have a double character. You can see them simply as the effects of other events in history: the effects of the hatred of the scribes and priests, the fears of Pilate; but on the other hand, you can see them for what they are in themselves and for us: you can see them as the struggle with the darkness, the victory of evil, the way back to life. And in that sense, they are the fulfilment of all humanity's dreams. They do what the human heart has always longed, and must always long, to do. And therefore, when we think about them, we must see them not just as something done for us, but as something that we, too, in our turn and in our different ways are meant to do.

The Pain of Christ and the Sorrow of God

"So Jesus came ... to a plot of land called Gethsemani."
We begin with the agony in the garden: What has that
to tell us about our own lives, our own struggles, our own
sorrows and sins?

The first thing it tells us is a thing of comfort. And He
prayed: "Father, if it be possible, let this chalice pass from
me" (Matt. 26:39, DR). It was for this, it was to drink this
cup, that He had come on earth; and yet now He prays that
He may not have to drink it. He prays to be released from
His destiny. We sometimes think of the saints as though
they lived in a world very remote from ours, as though they
were free from our struggles and tensions and fears, as though
they were able to give up home and friends, yes, and life
too, without a struggle, without any shrinking, without any
heartbreak. How wrong we are! " 'Father, let this chalice
pass from me.' ... And his sweat became as it were drops
of blood [see Luke 22:44, DR]. 'Father, if it be possible ...' "
Whatever else holiness may mean, it cannot mean that we
are expected to take every pain, every sorrow, as though it
were no pain or sorrow at all. "My soul is sorrowful even
unto death" (Matt. 26:38, DR).

What, then, does holiness mean?

Nevertheless, He goes on: "Not my will but thine be
done" (Luke 33:42). Holiness is not a question of what we
feel: it is a question of what we *will*. "Thy will be done." We
say it so often: if we could say it without any reservations,
wholeheartedly, we would be saints. A saint can fear his
destiny and want to escape it; he can pray to be released
from it; he can be heartbroken because of it; but because

he is a saint, he puts all his fears and his prayers and his sorrows into God's hands. *Not my will but Thine be done.* And it is by doing *that* that he shows how much he loves God. It is because he does *that* that he becomes a perfect instrument for God's purposes, becomes filled with power, the power that can help to save and heal the world. For the only thing that can heal the world is love.

But now, let us note another thing. This agony of our Lord and the prayer that expresses it: these are not something quite apart from what had gone before; they are the supreme expression of all that had gone before. From beginning to end of His life, He has one purpose only: "My meat is to do the will of him that sent me" (John 4:34, Knox). And therefore, every act in His life is an act of loving obedience; every act expresses that same prayer, "Not my will but Thine be done"; and therefore, every act is part of the story of redemption.

And so we come to the second thing that this scene in the garden can teach us. The unfolding story of God's love for man is not an affair merely of *great* events. The soil of today is made up of the innumerable tiny leaves and wisps of dust that were borne on the winds of the past. And the world's story, too, is the outcome not only of great or heroic deeds but of the innumerable unnoticed actions in the lives of simple folk. What we are to see in this prayer of our Lord is this: that the value of human actions does not depend on their importance. It depends ultimately on one thing: the degree to which we see them and love them as part of God's *will*; the degree to which we turn them into love.

There is a phrase that expresses that fact: the sacrament of the present moment. What does the phrase mean? We say a sacrament is an outward sign of inward grace. We are familiar with outward signs of inward states or experiences—the heightened color, for instance, that shows joy or anger or excitement—and a sacrament is something visible like that, but it shows a *divine* activity going on within the soul, the touch of God's hand.

And how can the present moment, each moment as it comes, be a sacrament, not of course like the seven sacraments but in something of the same sort of way? Simply because every event—not only Christ's Passion but every event—can have a double aspect. Every event can be seen simply as a result of other events, a purely human thing; but it can be seen, too, as our Lord saw it: as God's will for us. And if we see it, and love it, like that, then it becomes something great and deep, something in which God's love and wisdom are active because we have made it an act of love, have made it part of the love story.

You go to visit a sick friend; you do the ordinary work of home or business; you face this pain or that sorrow: and these are human things, but they are more than that. Take them as coming from God, turn them, as Christ did, into acts of love of God's will; and then they become part of His Passion, part of the long series of events that, in the end, will save the world. When you say, I want to do this thing, not against God's will, not apart from God's will, but as God's will, then you are giving it to Him in such a way that He can make it His action and give it His power; and so it becomes a mighty instrument in the fulfilling of the love story.

But what of evil things? Those are not God's will? No, but even Satan is made to serve the purposes of God's kingdom in the end: even out of evil good may come and does come; and when evil things come upon us, still the suffering of those is God's will for us, that out of them He may bring good.

And how does all this come about? You can see the answer in the *human* love that we all know. When two people love each other deeply, they learn little by little to have, as it were, one single will: and it is that that makes them truly one; it is that that fulfills their love. And what brings that about? Their way of meeting, as a unity, all the small events of every day, turning them into the material of their mutual love and understanding.

So it is with man's love of God. What the great lovers of God tell us again and again is this: that we must not despise the *small* things, the small events of every day. On the contrary, it is through them that we can learn to share God's life because it is out of them that goodness is made. We cannot afford to be less humble than God: what this scene in the garden again shows us is indeed precisely the completeness with which God emptied Himself of His glory and took on Himself the form of a servant. He did not become man, and enter as man the stage of history, merely in order to perform one or two dramatic actions in the sight of the world. He took upon Himself the helplessness of a baby, the ways of a child, the daily tasks and troubles and fatigues of manhood in a poor home, the dread of suffering. We shall become like Him not by trying every now and then to do great and grandiose things for God but by trying all the time to do all the little things of life for God, to give each of those, in turn, its sacramental value.

Let us think first of the trials that come to all of us. Sometimes they are very great; sometimes perhaps we feel they are too great for us to bear. Then we must remember: we are not asked to accept them lightheartedly. We may pray to be delivered from them, but we must try to put everything in God's hands: Thy will be done, not mine. But we shall not in fact be able to copy our Lord there unless we have trained ourselves in the smaller things.

Think of the *small* trials and irritations and setbacks that come to us every day, and how we react to them, so often, as though they had nothing to do with religion, nothing to do with our way back to God, nothing to tell us of the loving and redeeming will of God. What, in fact, do we do? We grumble, we grow agitated and angry or else gloomy and depressed and hard; then we hurt other people as well as ourselves: we lose sight of the love story.

And then there is the other side: the small joys that come our way too—the visit of a friend, a success in something we have been planning, any of the ordinary good things of life, any of the things that go to make the earth lovely. Here, too, we forget that they can be sacramental. Whatever it is that the moment brings us, of joy or of sorrow, we are to try to copy our Lord: we are to take it as an expression of God's will for us; and we are to try to love it—that is, to take it, if not gladly, at any rate willingly, readily—as His will, as part of the love story. Then we shall begin to live in God, and we shall have a part in His redeeming work in the world.

Omnia in manu Dei sunt, "all things are in the hands of God": that is the thing that the great lovers of God are always trying to make us see. But no, we have our own ideas, our own ambitions, our own view of how things ought to be and of what things we ought to do. O my soul, wrote St. Teresa, leave God to accomplish His will in you. And another great seeker after God used to say, "I *spoil* everything." We spoil everything because we cannot manage to will what God wills. We spoil everything. Even when we try generously to do something for God, we may spoil everything, because we think we know better than He; because we cannot leave the results in His hands; we cannot leave it to Him to decide what the success or the failure shall be. We spoil everything because, in our shortsightedness and our crudity, we try to serve God's ends with unworthy means. We spoil everything because we think of success and failure as the world thinks of them; we cannot learn from the folly of the Cross. We spoil everything because in everything that we do, there is self-will: we think of ourselves and not of God, not of love. Even in our trying to be good Christians, we can spoil everything because we think of *our* success or *our* failure, of what *we* have done or failed to do, and so we are depressed or elated about ourselves, and we forget God, we forget love.

No, all things are in the hands of God. You must do your planning for the morrow; you must make the efforts required of you; you must think out your problems and act as you think best; but then leave God to accomplish His will in you; make the moment as it comes and passes a love gift to the unsleeping love of God. He has care of you all, your Father who is in Heaven. Small things and big things, the sorrows and the joys: take them from Him and give them back into His hands with thanksgiving. *Not my will but Thine be done.*

Lent is a time when we are asked to share in a particular way in the Passion of our Lord—to share in it through penance, because penance, self-denial, is a way of training ourselves to choose love instead of selfishness. And behind all the particular forms of self-denial that we may choose for ourselves, behind and far deeper than these, there is precisely the self-denial of taking fully and wholeheartedly what the moment brings to us of vexation or labor—the people who put heavy demands on our patience, the work that is hard and unrewarding, the duty that has no appeal for us—of taking all these things as they come to us and accepting them fully and turning them fully into the acts of love that they ought to be.

There is one thing more. Where troubles and hardships are concerned, we do well to think of our own as little as possible, and then only in comparison with our Lord's. We are very wrong if we despise small things because they are small. At the same time, we are very wrong if, when they are painful, we forget that they are small — a tiny drop that can be of value at all only when it is poured into the brimming cup of His Passion like the drop of water poured into the wine at Mass. You remember the words of the Angel of the Agony in *The Dream of Gerontius*:

> Jesu, by that shuddering dread which fell on thee;
> Jesu, by that cold dismay which sickened thee;
> Jesu, by that pang of heart which thrilled in thee;
> Jesu, by that mount of sins which crippled thee;
> Jesu, by that sense of guilt which stifled thee;
> Jesu, spare these souls which are so dear to thee.[1]

It is by those things that we must measure the little vexations that come to us day by day.

But you remember too — and this must be our final thought and our final lesson — you remember how the Gospel goes on to tell us that after His prayer there came an angel from Heaven, strengthening Him. So it will be for us, too, in our small measure. When we are self-willed and thinking only of ourselves, we find anxiety and fear

---

[1] John Henry Newman, "The Dream of Gerontius," lines 836–844.

and gloom and restlessness; but in His will is our peace. You have to say with Christ the prayer of Christ: "Not my will but Thine." Then, from that sacramental act, there will flow into your soul, as though at the touch of a mighty spirt, the strength of Christ's peace, that peace that surpasses understanding, the peace that can soothe and heal and strengthen the soul even in the midst of sorrow.

And more than that. This access of strength is like the touch of a mighty spirit because indeed it takes us into another and greater world. These spirits inhabit a world greater immeasurably than ours: the world of infinite horizons, the land of the everlasting hills. But we, too, are meant to be citizens of it; and this is the way. Without the sense of God's will, we narrow down our lives to the material world. We are like misers crouching over their hoards and never seeing the skies. Indeed, we may narrow our prison still further, seeing in everything only the image of ourselves. But once we are made aware of the greatness of events as expressions of God's love, once we see and live their sacramental value, then we are liberated into a greater life. The winds of eternity blow about us, and the infinite skies are our home, and we, too, walk the eternal hills.

Let us try then, during this Lent, to learn this lesson from our Lord's agony: the love of God's will, the sacrament of the present moment. It is not a question of feelings, of never being sad at what God sends us: we are not to try to be greater than Christ Himself. It is a question of learning to see all events, even the smallest, for what they most deeply are: steps in the story of God's love for man. And if we can learn to do that, then we shall go on to play our small but important part in the unfolding of the story: we shall make all the small events of life things of value for the world as well as for ourselves, by seeing God's love in them, and so taking them lovingly from His hands and leaving the success or the failure of what we do in His hands. So we shall enter with Him into that strengthening of soul that is our need in every time of stress, and that deep and lasting and unfathomable peace of soul that is the quality of all true greatness, the quality of all those who have found the meaning of life by following in the footsteps of the Prince of Peace.

2

The Betrayal

And while they were at table he said, "Believe me, one of you is to betray me." They were full of sorrow, and began to say one after another, "Lord, is it I?"

—Matthew 26:21–22, Knox

As we follow the course of our Lord's Passion, we find in it many betrayals, many different kinds of betrayal; and we have much to learn from them. We find Him betrayed, in one way, by Peter, crouching over the fire before dawn, and by the other disciples, who fled from Him in the hour of crisis. We find a deeper betrayal on the part of the Jewish people, who turned against the man who had loved them, and who now cried, "His blood be upon us and upon our children" (Matt. 27:25, Knox). There is a greater betrayal still in the conduct of the priests, whose office it was to lead the people to God, and God to the people, but who in fact conspired to kill the God they should have worshipped. And then there is the greatest betrayal of all: the betrayal of Jesus by the man who was His follower and His friend and who betrayed Him with a kiss.

These things can tell us much about our own lives. Notice, first of all, the reactions of the Apostles: He cannot mean one of us. "Surely it cannot be I, Lord." Should we, too, say the same sort of thing? Yet let us look at our own lives in the light of these failures. Every sin is a form of betrayal.

First of all, there is the failure of Peter and the flight of the other Apostles. Why did they do it? The answer is clear enough: they were afraid. In the garden, they were afraid quite simply for their skins: the clatter of steel from the guards put them into a panic; they lost their heads. Peter follows our Lord to the high priest's house, but there, alone, in strange and hostile surroundings, he cannot meet the maidservant's question. There is something here of the fear that can go so deep, the fear of social embarrassment. "I tell you, I never set eyes on the man" (see Matt. 26:72).

In the last chapter, we were thinking of the importance of small things. Let us think of them again here. Perhaps we have never denied Christ in any grave way; but we are not always faithful to His teaching. We deny in our conduct what we affirm with our lips. And is it not sometimes precisely through fear? Is it not sometimes because we are afraid that being loyal to our beliefs will bring us discomfort or hardship or pain? I ought to act in this way or that way, but if I do, I shall lose my job, or lose my friend, or not be able to enjoy this, or be forced to endure that; and I don't want to. And so, leaving Him, we flee.

Or again, sometimes we feel that we ought to speak out for our principles; we ought to say clearly what we know to be true; but we shall not be popular if we do. We shall be laughed at. The company we are in is hostile to all that sort of thing; it is so much easier to pretend we agree with them. "I tell you, I never set eyes on the man."

And let us note at once: Why were the disciples so weak? Because they were not prepared. They had not thought it would be like this at all; they were expecting the coming of the kingdom in a very different way. And we, too, can be unprepared, though with so much less excuse. We can be unprepared in the sense that we have not tried to understand our Faith fully, have not tried to see as fully as we might the way it affects the ordinary affairs of life, the way it cuts across so much that is taken for granted in a non-Christian society. Still more, perhaps, we are unprepared because we have not really learned to know our Lord, have not really tried to live with Him day by day and year by year, and so we have not come to share His mind, to be prepared in mind beforehand to act as He would have us act. Like the disciples in the garden, we have not prayed enough; we have been content to slumber instead of praying; and so we are caught unawares like them and lose our heads.

But what of the Jewish people who turned against Him so suddenly: What lesson is there for us there? What does it mean, this sudden change of heart? It means that their allegiance was never more than skin deep. They loved Him, these people who had seen His miracles and heard His wise words and watched His gentleness and patience and power. They loved Him, oh yes, but only in that shallow, emotional sort of way that makes people follow the popular idol of the moment. They had not learned to *know* Him, to understand Him or His message; they had not learned that deep faith and dogged devotion that can withstand all assaults unmoved. And we have to ask ourselves now: How deep is *our* love? How deep are *our* faith and devotion?

The Pain of Christ and the Sorrow of God

Would we, too, be swayed in a moment of crisis by popular agitation? Do we find that at the first hint of ridicule, or the first argument against the Faith, we lose all our assurance, we feel our faith tottering, and perhaps, for a time at least, throw it all over?

And let us notice the fullness, the vehemence, of this betrayal: "His blood be upon us and upon our children." The enemy you are most bitter about is always the one who was once your friend. And let us notice the terrible sequel: "His blood be upon us ..." and it was, and has been, to the present day. And so it always is that sin produces its own inexorable consequences; the suffering comes—upon us or upon others—and even in small things the same, in degree, is true.

And so again the lesson: we cannot afford to let our knowledge and love of God remain on the surface of our lives, remain a merely emotional thing or a thing of outward routine. We must dig down deep and find God in the very depths of the spirit and learn to know Him there and there adore Him, so that His presence will abide in us, more real to us than our own selves. And then, in the time of temptation, we shall stand firm.

And what of the priests and the scribes? Let us say only this of them: that it was they who should most clearly have understood the credentials of Christ, yet it was they who sought to destroy Him. There is such a thing as culpable ignorance, culpable blindness. And are we always free of that? Or do we find, if we really look at our own hearts, that sometimes we try not to see the finger of God pointing out our way to us, try not to hear the voice of God asking a service of us. Psychologists talk of the process of rationalization: we persuade ourselves into thinking there are solid reasons for doing what we want to do, when really in our hearts we know the reasons all point the other way. We need to be on our guard against that kind of betrayal: resisting the known truth is not one of the lighter sins. So once again, we have to make God the guest of the deep places in the spirit; and learn to hear His voice there.

And then we come finally to the supreme betrayal, to Judas. And what we have to realize here is this: that for us as Catholics, all the betrayals we have been thinking of must necessarily be colored by the sin of Judas, must necessarily be *that* sort of a betrayal too—because we are His friends. We cannot claim, like the priests, that we had never accepted Him. We cannot claim, like the Jews, that we had not really known Him. We cannot even claim, like the Apostles, that we had not fully understood His personality and His mission. We have been of His household, and He of ours; He has come to us and made His abode with us; if we betray Him, we betray Him with a kiss.

But there is another sense in which those terrible words can be true of us too. You remember how our Lord spoke of those who refused to give food to the hungry and drink to the thirsty, refused to clothe the naked and give shelter to the homeless. You remember how He said that in doing this to His poor, they were, in fact, doing it to Him. And we have to ask ourselves whether in any way we are like that; whether we, too, are perhaps very righteous, very regular in fulfilling our own church duties but deaf to the cries of our neighbors, deaf to the distresses of our fellow men. To be that is always wrong, for anyone; it is always a betrayal of all that Christ stands for, all that He came to do. But for us to do it, as Christians, is more than a betrayal: we betray even while we pretend to love and serve; we betray the Son of Man with a kiss.

What moral, then, must we draw from all this? There are four points we might consider.

First, let us use this Lent to look into ourselves more carefully and candidly than before, to recognize and to understand our sinfulness more deeply, to see our betrayals for what they are. And having done that, let us be not like Judas whom pride drove to stubbornness and despair, but like Peter, who found in his fall the way to humility and a greater love. Let us see what we have done, and be deeply sorry, and know our need of Christ's power if we are not to do the same thing again. That is a great step forward; and if we can do that, we shall have brought good out of evil. It was after Peter had betrayed and been forgiven and learned his powerlessness apart from Christ that he became, in real fact, the Rock on which the Church was built.

Secondly, let us remember sometimes in this light the words of the Our Father: "Forgive us our sins as we forgive them that sin against us" (see Luke 11:4). What mountains we make of the small ways in which others disappoint or betray us! Let us see them in the light of the way we treat Christ; and so perhaps we shall grow out of our pettiness and learn to be greater of heart.

Thirdly, let us remember often the kinds of betrayal we have been considering: the betrayal from fear or social diffidence, the betrayal from shallowness of faith, the betrayal from self-deception. And let us do what we can to guard against them. We need to be *strengthened*. In Lent, God asks of us prayer and penance. And one of the effects of penance is precisely to strengthen the will against future assaults; and one of the effects of prayer is to strengthen the mind, to teach us to know in our hearts with certain, unshakable knowledge, that our Redeemer lives, that apart from Him there is no meaning to life, that the one thing that matters, in the end, is to have found Him and been faithful to Him.

And so, finally, let us think often of the Cross of Love, and of these betrayals of Love, in order to increase our own love: our love, first of all, of Him whom we have helped to betray; but our love also of our fellow men for whom He suffered and whom He loves. It was, you remember, after He had announced the betrayal at the Supper and Judas had gone out that He gave them the new commandment: "that you love one another as I have loved you" (John 15:12).

The Pain of Christ and the Sorrow of God

If we have betrayed Him — as, indeed, we all have — then we can find no better way to tell Him of our sorrow, and to repair as far as possible the damage done, than by fulfilling that commandment. For so we share, not with the betrayers but with the betrayed; not with what they did but with what He came on earth to do: we share in His healing of the world.

Is it I, Lord? The answer, for each of us, must be yes; but that answer is not final. It is for us to follow the way of St. Peter: to find in our very sinfulness a deeper understanding and a stronger love. So, in the end, we may be able, please God, to answer Christ's question as Peter answered it at the last: "'Simon, son of John, lovest thou me?'... 'Yea, Lord, thou knowest that I love thee'" (John 21:15).

3

THE SCOURGING

Then Pilate took Jesus and scourged him.

—John 19:1, Knox

L et us now think, as reverently and lovingly as we can, of this next scene in our Lord's Passion and again see what lessons it holds for our everyday lives.

We can distinguish here three moments: our Lord is first stripped of His garments; then He is scourged; and then finally they put on Him a scarlet cloak, in mockery of His kingship, and a crown of thorns, and they cry, "Hail, king of the Jews."

First the taking of His garments: He was always the poor man of Galilee, but this is the ultimate poverty. You think of St. Francis, who, when he wanted to have done completely with his life of worldliness, threw away even his clothes and, naked, followed the naked Christ. This, then, is the poverty of Christ.

And then the scourging: and in this intensity of physical suffering many have seen a special atonement for our fleshly sins, for the way in which, instead of ruling the flesh, we let the flesh rule over us. This is the redeeming chastity of Christ.

And finally, the mockery of His kingship: and in these days we keep a special feast of Christ the King, but we deny in our lives this affirmation of loyalty whenever, in fact, we go against the rule of Christ, whenever we set up our own self-centered will against the will of Christ. It is this that He suffers, then, in the soldiers' mockery, and for this that He atones by setting aside His rule and accepting this ultimate rebellion from His creatures.

Poverty, chastity, obedience: they have a special meaning for those who vow themselves to the religious state and freely give up property and family life and the freedom of action; but they have a meaning, too, for every Christian: not in the same way but in another way, they are elements in every Christian life that is a true following of Christ.

Blessed are the poor in spirit. There is something about poverty itself that makes the poor very near and dear to the heart of Christ. Not that poverty that is, in fact, a crushing burden of penury, a constant anxiety and anguish of spirit, but the poverty that means a very modest way of life, a simplicity, a lack of great possessions. About that sort of poverty there is something Christlike. Why is it? You find the answer in another Gospel phrase: "the *cares* of this world" (Mark 4:19). Wealth can so easily mean a distraction from God, can so easily mean an absorption in the things of this world. It may be by way of anxiety and fear of loss; it may be by way of absorption in the pleasures, the amusements, the indulgences that money can buy; in any case, the essentials are the same: it is easy to be wholly taken up with the things of this world and to forget God, to live the life of every day apart from God. We have all seen a dog or a cat taking its tidbits into a remote corner to enjoy them there alone, safe from other claimants, safe from distractions. It is very easy to be like that with our worldly goods. But poverty of spirit touches more than material things: it concerns all our possessions, all our gifts. You remember the prodigal son, who asked, "Father, give me the portion that belongs to me"; and he went from home into a far country—the dog taking his bone into the corner—to live riotously (see Luke 15:12–13). We tend to do that with all our gifts, whatever they are. You may have great personal gifts—great charm or beauty or wit or intelligence—and you realize the power or the pleasure they can bring you. And so you become absorbed in them; you forget that they come from God, that they are God's gifts, to be used for Him. You take them to a far country, away from Him and enjoy them there, simply for your own ends, forgetting that other life, that supreme love, that is your home. You may have great gifts of another sort: the joys of marriage, of friendship, of music, of any creative work. These, too, can lead you into the far country; these too can make you forget God your home.

Now you notice how the story of the prodigal son goes on. These things all turn in the end into husks. The one way to miss happiness is to set out to find it like that. But then the son returns in sorrow to his father's house; and then the things he has been misusing to his own misery find their proper place: then there is music and feasting and dancing, the rich garments, and the fatted calf. It is not these things that are wrong: it is the way we use them so often that is wrong. And we use them wrongly precisely because we use them as though they were ours exclusively; as though we were the masters; as though God had no say in the matter. That is what we have to reverse if we want to be poor in spirit: we have to make these things not a distraction from God but a part of our life with God. So St. Paul tells us we should use the things of this world *quasi non utentes*, as though we were not using them. And what does he mean? He does not mean that we must try not to love them. He means that we must try not to love them apart from God, apart from God's will, apart from the thought that they are God's gift to us, and a gift that may be withdrawn. So you find in the saints — in St. Francis, for example — who give up everything: they give up the *possession* of everything, the proprietorship of everything, not the *love* of everything. On the contrary, it is when they have thrown away all their possessions that their love can so increase as to include all things, that they can become all things to all men, and indeed to all creatures. It is not for nothing that so many of the saints have their pet animals.

So we must try, like them, to be poor of spirit. Think of something, or somebody, you love very much. How are you to be poor in spirit about that possession? First, you must train yourself to think of it as a gift from God, something to which, of yourself, you have no right. Then you must try to love it, not away from God, not as a different part of your life from your life of religion, but as part of your love of Him, often thanking Him for giving it to you, and often trying to put it into His hands, to say that you want your enjoyment of it to be according to His will, not yours. And so you will learn gradually not to be possessive about it; you will learn to care and yet not care, to love and yet be free, to have nothing and yet possess all things.

When you think thus of poverty of spirit during Lent, you can see how the prayer and penance that are then expected of the Christian can help you. Pray about all the gifts that God has given you, material and otherwise, and ask Him to help you to use them for Him and not selfishly and exclusively for yourself. Ask Him to teach you to see Him in all things, and all things in Him, so you will achieve something of the vision of the saints, for whom all things are filled with God's presence and eloquent of God's love.

And then penance, self-denial: if you give alms, you are training yourself to be carefree about money. If you go out of your way to be generous with what worldly goods you have, you are training yourself to see them as God's possessions and not as your own; and so you are using them, not in riotous living in a far country, but as part of the music and dancing of the prodigal's return, the festivities of home. And in doing that, you are also doing something deeper: you are doing something to share in the poverty, the redeeming poverty, of our Lord. And when your own self-denials bring you suffering, or when God, in His wisdom, asks suffering of you, the suffering of privation or loss, then you will know that you have thus a small part in this sorrowful and glorious moment of the Passion and that, in some small way, you are following, naked, the naked Christ.

Think now of the second moment, the scourging of our Lord. If there were no sin in man, human nature would be a harmony. We know all too well how it is in fact: we are pulled different ways; we find the flesh rebelling against the spirit; we find, like St. Paul, that we fail to do what we want to do—the flesh is too strong for us. Our best impulses come to nothing because we give way to laziness or love of comfort; our lives are made ugly because we give way to greed or impurity. What are we to do? Our duty is to restore the harmony as far as we can; and here again Lent can help us. Whenever we deny the flesh, we strengthen the spirit; we make it easier to avoid those sins in the future. And as with poverty, so here, too, we must see the thing in a larger context. Mind and body affect each other. It is not only that a lack of harmony between them leads us into sins of the flesh: it is also that the tyranny of the flesh, of senses and emotions, can harm the mind, can cloud our vision and our judgment.

"Blessed are the clean of heart: for they shall see God" (Matt. 5:8, DR); but to be clean of heart means also to be clear in vision, to be candid and genuine and to see things as they are and not as our senses and emotions would like them to be. You know how passion and greed and jealousy can distort the vision. That is what we have to avoid, and that is what chastity of heart can help us to do. And so, when you school yourself to resist the sham and shoddy and meretricious, when you force yourself to see things truly, to be really candid and to worship the truth; when you train the senses to play their proper part in the whole personality's search for the knowledge of the truth and the love of the good and the beautiful; then you are being clean of heart; you are restoring something of the original harmony; you are bringing humanity nearer to God's ideal for it. But again, you are doing something more. For this, too, is not to be achieved except by labor and self-denial and perhaps much suffering; and so again you can take part with Christ. You can feel that in this moment of the Passion, too, you are with Him: you can not only undo some of the evil done; you can take an active and creative share in this moment of His redeeming pain.

And then, finally, the crown, the cloak, the mockery of the kingship: What of these? The Word of God emptied Himself of His glory, humbled Himself in obedience to love, when He took to Himself the nature of man. But here the humiliation goes far beyond that: here He is robbed of what was His right precisely as man, the kingship over men. And still He accepts; still He obeys. And as it is His obedience that includes all the rest and makes of all the rest an act of love and of redemption, so for us, too, it is this element of obedience that turns other virtues into acts of love and worship, so that morality finds its fulfillment by becoming religion. For the monk, the third vow includes the other two. For the Christian living in the world, the spirit of obedience to God's will includes poverty of spirit and cleanness of heart and ensures that they shall be what they are, not for their own sake, but for the sake of love.

And how is this, the essential quality of the Christlike life, to be learned? Again, by repeated efforts, such efforts as Lent particularly demands of us, to love God's will: efforts to go beyond the bare letter of the law, the minimum of morality, and to make gifts to God of our freedom.

Let us recall the three freedoms of which St. Paul tells us: you can be free in the sense of not being another man's slave, but that is not enough to make you fully free, for there is the bondage of sin, the sort of slavery we have been thinking about, which makes us do the things we want not to do. To break our way through that bondage is the second freedom. But still we may not be fully free. There is the bondage of law, the bondage that consists in obeying the law, not gladly and willingly, but reluctantly, feeling the law as an external pressure weighing down upon us and making us go against our desires. And how to break through that final bondage? Not by repudiating the law, which would only mean a return to the bondage of sin, but by learning to see the law for what it is, the will of love, and, through our own love, learning to love that will of love. For love means wanting to do the will of what you love. And so obedience becomes a free choice and act: it becomes free because it becomes synonymous with love. And that is the final freedom, the freedom of the sons of God.

And so, whenever we go against one part of our many-leveled nature for the sake of love; whenever we deny ourselves a self-centered pleasure or a possessiveness, train ourselves to poverty or cleanness of heart, for the sake of love, then we are joining in the humility of Christ's obedience, the obedience that won the world back to love.

Let us think of these things then as we prepare to follow our Lord on the way to Calvary. And, thinking of them, let us try to put them into practice in our own lives, in our own ways. Learn to be poor in spirit about the particular things, the particular gifts, the particular blessings that your particular life brings you. Learn to be clean of heart, to restore the balance between body and spirit, in the ways that particularly affect you, your particular temptations, your particular blindnesses, your particular twists of vision or cheapnesses of heart. Learn to go beyond the letter of the law and to make gifts, love gifts, to God of your own freedom, so as to find your true freedom in love of His will. Then you will be better prepared to go with Him to His Cross, for you will have done much to make it not only His Cross but yours. You will have a share with Him in His redeeming pain and sorrow, but you will also have learned many things: that the road to Calvary is also and at the same time the road to Paradise.

4

THE STILLNESS OF MARY

Now there stood by the cross of Jesus his mother.

—John 19:25, DR

When you tread again, with Christian tradition, the road to Calvary, you recall the meeting between Jesus and His Mother; but you notice that there is no word spoken, no action done. It is the same at the end: she stands at the foot of the Cross, but she is silent and still. And indeed, what you notice about the story of the Passion as a whole is the striking contrast between the quiet stillness of those who love Him and the ceaseless activity of His enemies. The priests are called in haste to the midnight session of the Sanhedrin. The traitor Judas runs to and fro. There is the tramp of the Temple guards and the Roman soldiery; the agitation of Pilate; the bustle of the palace, probably the unprecedented upset of a visit by night from the high priest. Over all, there is the clamor and movement, the shouting and disturbance, of the Jewish mob. But the central figures are still.

Jesus allows Himself to be led hither and thither, yes, but in Himself He is stillness; He scarcely speaks. Mary follows to the end, but again she is silent; she does nothing: she stands motionless, rigid, supporting her Son. There is something—something absolutely essential—that we must learn from her. Her vocation was to be a mother, wrapped up in the work of her Son. And for many years, for thirty years, that meant a life of ceaseless activity, a life of hard work, for Him. But then the time came when she was no longer needed: He had to begin His own work in the world. And so, as you see in the Gospels, she withdraws into the background. You hear almost nothing of her, until the end. And then she is there; she is with Him—not to work now, not to be active, only to love and suffer and be still. You remember her words in *The Man Born to Be King*:

> When he was small, I washed and fed him; I dressed him in his little garments and combed the rings of his hair. When he cried, I comforted him; when he was hurt, I kissed away the pain; and when the darkness fell, I sang him to sleep. Now he goes faint and fasting in the dust, and his hair is tangled with thorns. They will strip him naked to the sun and hammer the nails into his living flesh, and the great darkness will cover him. And there is nothing I can do. Nothing at all.[2]

It is a terrible thing, a thing we must all at some time have suffered, that feeling that someone you love is suffering and you can do nothing to help. And yet these words of Mary are not said in despair. And we, too, if we have to say something like them, must not despair; we shall be wrong if we despair. This is the first lesson we are to learn from her.

---

[2] Dorothy L. Sayers, *The Man Born to Be King: A Play-Cycle on the Life of Our Lord and Saviour Jesus Christ* (San Francisco: Ignatius Press, 1990), 289.

There are two sorts of activity. There is outgoing activity: the healing work of the hands, the comforting word, the little service that can bring consolation; and sometimes these are impossible. But there is another sort of activity, a purely inward activity, and this is always possible and always healing. And this is the activity of thought and of love and of the lovely child of these two, which we call sympathy. You may have to say, "There is nothing I can do, nothing of outward activity." You need never say, purely and simply, "There is nothing I can do." It is our Lady herself who, later on in the same reconstruction of the Passion, says, "Be still, sister, be still: we have no need of words, my Son and I."

Be still: the stillness and the silence of Mary are the signs not of defeat but of intense and creative activity. There are times when outward busyness only makes matters worse, when, though it may bring you yourself relief, it must be for the other, at best, ineffectual and, at worst, an additional exacerbation of suffering.

Be still: there are times when, if only you are still enough and wise enough, you can learn that all these outward activities of themselves cannot heal, that only love can heal. There is nothing that Mary can do or say; no, but they have no need of words, her Son and she: it is love that heals. And so, when you follow with love and sorrow this story of the Cross, and you want to help; you want to do something for the pain and the sorrow; you want to comfort, never think that there is nothing you can do. Think deeply and love deeply, and then you will have no need of words: your sympathy, your co-suffering, will go straight from your own heart to the heart of Christ. Rather, it was already there as He trod the way of the Cross those many centuries ago, was already there to comfort Him as His silent Mother was there to comfort Him, and is with Him now and for all eternity as part of His bliss. There is never nothing that you can do.

And the same thing is true if you are thinking of the sorrow and suffering with which the world is filled today. If your heart is with Christ, who suffered for the sins that have made this suffering, then you will long to do something to lessen it, to heal, and to help; but perhaps you will have the bitterness of knowing that as far as outward activity is concerned, there is nothing you can do. Never mind. The same thing is true: you can co-suffer in your heart, and it is love that heals.

We are not blind materialists, to suppose that only material things can really help the sorrow of the human heart. On the contrary, we know how often those material things themselves are powerless to affect anything but the surface, how often indeed they can make the suffering worse when they are not the fruit of love. We are not blind materialists, to suppose that physical distance is an insuperable barrier to help and healing. On the contrary, we know the power of the human spirit to conquer space as it can conquer time. We know, above all, how the spirit that is one with the spirit of Christ can bring from Him the same healing touch that physically, long ago in Palestine, brought life and joy and wholeness to the world. Be comforted then; for it is always in your power to bring comfort to others. That is the first lesson we can learn from Mary at the foot of the Cross.

But there is a second and a deeper lesson. It is the en-emies of Christ who are active. And some of that activ-ity, the thronging and tumult of the mob, is thoughtless; and thoughtless activity is always barren and, in the end, harmful. But some of the activity is not thoughtless; it is the result of thought, but of thought apart from God, the result of shallowness and shortsighted stupidity, or, at its worst, of pride and hatred and malevolence; and that sort of activity is always evil in the end and always, in the end, must bring deep evil and suffering on the world. We have seen before how action for our neighbor can be a duty. We cannot claim to love God unless we love our fellow men, and that means willing their good as our own, and that means doing what we can for them when they are in need or distress. But there is the other side of the picture. If you think that action alone is all that matters, action without thought, without the deep wisdom that you learn from God, then you will make matters worse; you will do harm in the end and not good. Action without prayer is blind.

You look back on the history of the world, and again and again you find the same thing exemplified. It is not the active and thoughtless who bring good to the world; it is the contemplatives and those whose action springs from contemplation. You will find activity among the Huns and the Goths, who swept over Europe like a tidal wave and destroyed a civilization. You will find activity in those who tried to serve good ends by ill-considered means, evil means whose evil they had not noticed, and so brought ruin to the things they tried to serve. You will find activity among those who produce short-term plans and policies and blueprints that will fulfill an immediate economic or political end, without considering the end of all these ends, which is man's immortal destiny. Too often it is here that you have the counterpart of the Jewish mob or the scheming priests and scribes. Too often Christ is betrayed by action without thought, without prayer. It is not thus that the world is saved. "Be still, sister, be still." The history of the world is very largely a history of man's thought; and where the thought is superficial, and still more where it is godless and proud, disaster follows. "Where there is no vision, the people perish" (Prov. 29:18, KJV).

No need to underline the relevance of all this for our world of today—a world of speed and frenzied activity; a world that thinks too exclusively in terms of the science that can tell us how, instead of the wisdom that tells us what and why. Let us indeed salute with reverence the activity of those who give their energies to the service, to the saving, of humanity. Still more, let us honor the love that so often is the driving force behind that activity. But at the same time, let us not be deluded: it is not thought about means that will save the world unless, first of all, there has been thought about ends, about the one end of all, which is God. Where there is no vision, there, no matter how great and how noble the activity, the people will perish in the end.

What does this vision mean? We were thinking before of the line of the poet, "Teach us to care and not to care," but now we must add what follows: "Teach us to sit still."[3] Vision means seeing the end in the beginning, seeing always the depths and the heights, seeing the history of man as a single whole and the nature of man in terms of a single destiny, seeing God. And we cannot do that unless we learn to be still. You remember how the carol tells us:

> He came all so still
> Where his mother lay,
> Like dew in April
> That falleth on the spray.

It is always thus that He, the uncreated Wisdom, comes into the hearts of men. To be still and silent, to listen and to learn, to allow the Spirit of God to inhabit and mold the soul: this is contemplation; and it is when action flows from this that it brings help and healing to the world.

Is this a rare and difficult thing? Rare, in fact, it may be, but it is the vocation of every man. Difficult it is in the sense that it puts demands upon the will, yes, but not in the sense that we need to be clever and learned to achieve it. On the contrary, it is not the simple and unlettered who say they cannot pray. They say their Rosary or their simple prayers day by day, and often they end by becoming great mystics, even though they remain unknown, and it may well be they, in their obscurity, who change the face of the earth. No, it is the educated and the well-read and the intelligent who sometimes say they cannot pray, cannot be men or women

---

[3] T. S. Eliot, "Ash Wednesday," stanza 1.

of prayer; and this is a terrible comment on our civilization. For if they are telling the truth, it means that our culture is not culture at all but the death of culture, not the way to wisdom but the destruction of wisdom. More probably, they are deceived by their surface life, the speed and restlessness that mark our common life, the inability to sit still. If we give in to that, then indeed we are lost. But we for whom the duty of prayer is a commonplace of our teaching, we who have constantly before us the example of the saints, whose activity was always the overflow of their prayer; we who have been shown so often the mortal effects of activity unconditioned by prayer, we at least should be clear what it is we have to do; we at least should make sure that in spite of the tempo of the modern world, we shall learn to be still.

That is what this story tells us, for our own lives and for the life of our world. "We have no need of words, my Son and I." When you begin to pray, perhaps you will need many words; it is like a friendship that is new. But if you go on faithfully, perhaps you will find the need of words grows less; perhaps you will tend more and more to use the same little set of words again and again, as is the way of lovers. And perhaps still later, that, too, will become unnecessary; you will be content to rest silently in His presence, like lovers who have reached the deep waters of wisdom and understanding together; you will have no need of words. And so you yourself will be safe in His arms; and you will be with Him, comforting Him in His sorrow and being glad with Him in His joy, not only because you are busy about many things for Him—though that, too, you will be, inevitably, so far as your strength and opportunity and His will permit—but primarily because you have chosen like another Mary the better part and it shall not be taken from you (see Luke 10:42).

But then, too, you will be with Mary, His Mother, at the very center of His work for the world, His healing of the world. For it is this that gives power to heal with Christ. It is love that heals. If you love this land of ours and sorrow for its present distresses; if you love Europe and its heritage of beauty and knowledge and wisdom; if you love the world, which is humanity's home, then of course you will want to work to save and heal and strengthen; and your love will give you the energy that can compass mighty works. But you must have the one thing necessary. You must make sure that the work is the fruit of vision. You must make sure that "you live, now not you, but Christ liveth in you" (see Gal. 2:20), because you have learned to be still and receive life and power from His hands.

It is not merely penance that the Church asks of us during Lent: it is extra prayer. And indeed, since prayer in our sin-blinded condition demands effort and energy, challenges our laziness and superficiality, our reluctance to leave the realm of the transitory for the kingdom of ends, we can very valuably combine the two commands. For what better penance could there be than to get up a little earlier every day so as to attend Mass, to go to some trouble to make a visit every day to the church, to make time every day for a Rosary or some other extra prayer? And if we do this in order to be with Mary, His Mother, in His Passion, if we do this in order to be still with her, absorbed in the tragedy and victory of His love, then we shall be entering into life ourselves, and also, whether it is in our power to be outwardly active or not, we shall be bringing life, in and through Him, to the world.

We shall be life bringers. You notice how, in this story, it is the activity of mob and priests and soldiers that brings death; it is they who call to death, they who cry, "Crucify Him, crucify Him!" And you notice too, in this modern world of ours, how with the breathless speed of life and the endless activity, the ceaseless change and movement, there goes a very different phenomenon: the will to death. Sometimes it is complete and explicit: a real desire for death, a real desire to have done with it all, to sleep. More often it is a kind of paralysis of the spirit, of the will: the sense of hopelessness that kills all initiative. Perhaps most commonly of all you find it in a diluted form: the personal life escapes it more or less completely — there there is hope and interest and initiative and creation — but that personal life is an oasis in a limitless desert. Outside its immediate confines there is despair, there is no hope for society, for the future of humanity. You seize what the personal life can give you for the moment, but for the rest, you remain convinced that humanity is steadily declining, that the world we have known, the civilization that nurtured us, is doomed and there is nothing to be done.

This is an immobility very different from the immobility of Mary, the immobility of the monk, of the man of vision, the man of prayer — the immobility, the stillness, in which life is born. This is the immobility of death. The twelfth and thirteenth centuries have the zest of Europe's springtime; the Renaissance has the color of high summer; in the Age of Reason there is something of the late maturity of autumn. But now winter lies heavy upon us, and it is difficult even to remember the thrill of spring. Our world is old; and how shall a world be born again? There is no answer save the answer given to Nicodemus (see John 3:4ff.).

Let us make no mistake. This will to death, this heaviness of spirit, this deep despair of life that cries out to the dark gods, "Crucify us, crucify us": this comes from the restlessness that is born of rootlessness. It is because of the lack of vision that the people perish; we have lost sight of the fountains of living water, and so there is not health or hope in us. And if you seek to remedy the situation by economic or political programs without seeking to heal the evil at its source, then inevitably you are beating the air. You can provide a brief sedative, an anesthetic; you cannot make the dry bones live.

"Be still, sister, be still: we have no need of words, my Son and I." To Mary, it was told at the beginning: "And thy own soul a sword shall pierce" (Luke 2:23, DR). The disciples were not prepared, but she was prepared. She had known beforehand something of how it would be, how it must be; and having seen her own vocation in her Son's, she was faithful to it to the end. But the end, which is the folly of the Cross—this was not the end for her Son, nor for her in her pre-vision, nor for us. She saw, through the anguish and helplessness of death, the renewal of life; through the savage winter, the coming of the spring. She saw, but more than that, she hastened its coming by the silence and stillness of her sorrow.

And so it must be for us. To us too, to our dying world, He will come all so still: He will come if, but only if, our world can learn sufficiently to be still and silent and adoring, can learn to return in quiet of soul to its source, can become again a contemplative world.

5

THE VALLEY OF THE SHADOW OF DEATH

And about the ninth hour Jesus cried
out with a loud voice … "My God, my
God, why hast thou forsaken me?"

—Matthew 27:46, Knox

If you are leading an ordinary, happy life, perhaps it is easy for you to believe in God's love. But suppose that something horrible happened to you, that you were put into a concentration camp and starved and tortured. Could you go on believing then? Is it even right for you to believe in God's love and be happy when the world is suffering so? These questions must now be considered. They will take us deeper into the problem of pain.

It is useless to speculate what we might do in such circumstances—only God knows that—but what we can do is prepare. We have seen how the disciples fled because they were unprepared; how our Lady was with her Son to the end because she was prepared. She had understood, as they had not, how the Cross is the way to the Kingdom, how death must precede resurrection, how it is out of the darkness that light is born.

Let us, first of all, try to see the picture as a whole. The world is filled with suffering. Why? Because the world is filled with sin, and sin always, inexorably produces suffering. Pride, greed, cruelty, lust: these things inflict suffering on others, and ultimately on the doer as well. Evil and suffering alike may well be handed on from generation to generation; the wheel inexorably turns; the world is plunged ever further into the darkness. But why does God allow the evil and the suffering it produces? First, because he is Love, and Love does not rule by violence; the power of free will is given, and it means the power to return hatred for love if we so choose. But secondly, you remember how the Church on Holy Saturday speaks of the primal sin as *felix culpa*, a blessed fault, because, through it, humanity has something of ineffable value that it could not have had otherwise. Had there been no sin, we would not have known that immense revelation of the depths of love that is the Cross; and, for our part, we would not have known the human response to it; we would not have been capable of that depth of love and understanding that only sorrow can bring to us. The divine truth is made clear to us in its human analogy; for human beings find, in their love of one another, that the deepest glory is that which comes of pain. Suffering, then, has a creative, a redemptive, role: wherever there is suffering in the world, there is the sorrow of God; and to share in the human suffering and the divine sorrow is to find the way to life in its fullness—not only for oneself but, in the end, for the world.

Sometimes people say, "Yes, I see how suffering can be good for us if we understand its purpose and accept it in the right way. But what of those who cannot understand—what of innocent children, of animals?" But we must remember, first, that such good is not limited to the conscious level; and we must not diminish God's power to bring good out of evil in His own time. Secondly, we are a family: we suffer because of one another, and also, unconsciously, we suffer for one another. Even the animal creation, made originally to find its fulfillment in the service of man, may have to be seen in its suffering as forming a part of that total return of the fallen world through darkness to the light, and as helping man, through the spectacle of its pain, to awareness of the deep problems. We are all a family; in a true sense, we are each responsible for all. Of Christ it was said that for our sake He was made sin (2 Cor. 5:21), and we, too, in our turn, are meant to share the sin and sorrow of the world in union with Him, that, out of that sharing, the sin and sorrow may be healed. Perhaps the problem of evil and pain can never be wholly solved; but evil and pain can be resolved: the darkness can be transformed into light. It is to that that we are called.

What, then, are we to do? How are we to learn, and so to be prepared, that our "faith fail not" (Luke 22:32, DR)? You remember how they once asked our Lord for a sign, and He told them that a sign should not be given them except the sign of Jonah the prophet (Matt. 12:38–39). For pride, for self-sufficiency, for the righteousness of conventionalized piety—there can be no other sign than that. For what the story of Jonah in the whale's belly is telling us in picture language is that pride will never learn what Christianity means until it has gone down into the darkness, and until it is left naked and helpless and without resources and so is thrown back into the arms of God. Why is it, people ask, that Catholicism is so ineffective in the world if its claims are true? And is not the answer that we Catholics, who represent the Church, are proud and self-reliant and conventionalized, content if we more or less keep the law of God, content if we are more or less respectable — and so we regard our goodness, such as it is, as *our* goodness? We never notice the egoism that lies at the root of it, poisoning everything; we never notice the reservations we place all the time on our service, on our self-giving, to God; we forget the cry of Gerontius as he sees himself truly for what he is, against the purity of Love:

> Take me away, and in the lowest deep
> There let me be.[4]

And so perhaps we go on placidly; and perhaps, if there came suddenly a terrible upheaval, a terrible cross, we should indeed be unprepared and we should fail. But, on the other hand, sometimes God in His pity uses a disaster of one sort or another precisely to sweep away all our illusions and bring us back to reality. It may be a terrible moral collapse that shakes us to our roots; it may be a loss of faith, of faith in God, of faith in ourselves, of faith in everything; it may be the pressure of external events, the collapse of a world about our ears. In one way or another, we can be left naked; we begin to see ourselves as we really are in our nothingness. We go down into the darkness; and there

---

[4] John Henry Newman, "The Dream of Gerontius," lines 103–104.

in that darkness we begin to cry, "Out of the depths" (Ps. 130:1). And then at last there is hope for us.

You remember some of the "harsh" sayings of our Lord: "Let the dead bury their dead"; "Unless a man hate his father and his mother ..."; "Sell all thou hast" (Matt. 8:22; see Luke 14:26; Matt. 19:21, DR). What are they telling us if not the same thing: you cannot serve God and mammon; you cannot be at the same time a Christian and a self-complacent egoist; you cannot claim to follow Christ if you give only half of yourself to Christ. There is no way to life except through death and rebirth: that rebirth in the Spirit, which means a full surrender of will, through love, to the will of the Spirit.

If we were wise, we could learn this for ourselves. But we are stupid, and sometimes God has to force it on our attention—has to lead us near to physical death, or mental disintegration, or moral collapse, or the death of faith. Sometimes we need the final horror; sometimes there is nothing left for us, as for Dante, but to be taken down to the abode of the "lost people" in order that our eyes may be opened: to realize the utter blank frozen emptiness that is Hell. Think of this when you go into the church on Good Friday with its empty tabernacle—no longer a home but only a house. And think then of the final terror of the Crucifixion, the final torment of the Cross: "My God, my God, why hast thou forsaken me?" (Matt. 27:46, DR). What did it mean?

In the universality of His love and His pity, Christ shared the sorrow and pain of every human being through the long story of mankind. He knew in His own heart every cry of pain and agony that had ever risen or would ever rise from the valley of human tears. But there is more than that. St. Paul tells us that Christ was *made sin* for our sake (2 Cor. 5:21), and perhaps we are to understand, not indeed that He became a sinner, but that He knew in His heart the ultimate torment of the sinner; knew what William Law called the second agony, the agony of emptiness and horror that is final separation from God. How indeed could He fail to know it, whose sympathy excluded nothing of human experience? But if so, He knew it with the one essential difference: He knew it, not like the lost people, with hatred in His heart; not, as it might be for us, with loss of all faith; but as the final act of sacrifice, and therefore as the last and thickest pall of darkness that precedes the dawn. It is the glory of *consummatum est* that follows: the work is complete, is perfected: I have conquered the world.

The last act of *sacrifice*: that is the lesson we have to learn. The death that leads to resurrection is not just a death, but a sacrificial death, a death turned into an act of love and self-giving. You have your pain and your sorrow, your anxieties, your personal problems, your moral lapses, perhaps your loss of faith. Turn these into the sign of Jonah the prophet. Use these to lead you down into the darkness. Take these to the altar of love and tumble them into His hands and ask *Him* to deal with them, like a little child taking a worthless piece of treasure trove as a gift to his mother.

And not merely your own sorrows and your own sins, but the sorrows and sins of the world: you who should be so powerful to heal them in the might of Love and who in fact are so powerless to do anything, take these too and give them to Him. Make these, too, an act of sacrificial love, suffering for them yourself in union with His sorrow; and so, having seen to the very depths of your own ineffectiveness, you will cease to be ineffective. You will begin to live, now not you, but Christ living in you.

Be comforted then. Perhaps God will allow you at some time to suffer what seems the final dereliction—not just a sharing in the *agony* of loss of God, as Christ could know it, but the *loss* itself, which He could never know. It may be a moral abyss from which you feel yourself wholly impotent to escape; it may be a sense of utter blankness: a loss of the faith that once explained life and made it happy, so that now everything seems meaningless. These states can sometimes be due to physical or mental exhaustion, essentially transitory: that does not mean that, while they exist, they are any the less real.

But if they come to you, refuse to despair: it may well be that this death is your way of life. Refuse to despair, and be comforted: it may well be that this death is the way that God's love has discovered for you of finding not the unreal conventionalized Christ who leaves your egoism intact but the real Christ, the Christ on the Cross, the Christ who is Love. Refuse to despair, and, on the contrary, take that gift, too, to the altar: put your very dereliction itself into Christ's hands; and sooner perhaps than you could hope, more richly, certainly, than you could dream, He will turn those waters of sorrow into the rich red wine of life.

For so, for you, as for Christ your Savior, the *lama sabachthani* will not be the last word; for you, as for Him, it will lead to the glorious cry, the *consummatum est*. For you, it will never again be necessary—or, unless you are very foolish, possible—to return to the shallow superficiality of conventionalized religion; your heart will have learned that you can begin to climb toward the heights. For what is perfected then, for you, is the grandeur and joy of complete liberation. You can shake off the deadly bondage of egoism, the cares and anxieties, the fears and greeds, the troubles and tensions, as a man frees his shoulders of an overwhelming burden. You can be free, unfettered, reborn, naked not now in the sense of bereft and helpless but with the freedom of the sons of the morning, glorying in the golden sunshine of God. It is not that you make less effort, have less concern for your duties in the world, for your care for those near to you, for your own soul. You try much harder; your concern is far greater and deeper. But you have put all these things in God's hands; you make the effort, but you leave the result to Him; you are patient, even with yourself; you are not disappointed, because you expect nothing of yourself; and so, in the words of the Eastern mystic, there is no more worry for you, not even about not being perfect.

Think of the saints, who found this way to life in the follow-ing of Christ, and you will see the second thing that inevi-tably follows. They are free, with the total freedom of the sons of God, because the false ego has been killed in them. Their hearts are fully opened to love, but the human heart is capable of infinity, and so the infinite life comes flooding in; the infinite power of God comes flooding in. And then there is nothing they cannot do. Like Paul, they live, not they, but Christ liveth in them; and, like Paul, they can do all things in him who strengthens them (Gal. 2:20; Phil. 4:13).

Think of the saints, but not in order to be discouraged, not in order to think that what is done in them is something rare and grandiose that can never be done in you. They are the heroes, yes, whom we admire from afar; but they began at the beginning, and we can begin at the beginning too—and leave it humbly to God to decide how far along the road we may go. We have been thinking of this death that leads to life in some of its more dramatic forms; but the same thing can be done in a much simpler and more ordinary fashion.

The same thing can be achieved through the humdrum events of the everyday life. The small pains and troubles that come to you day by day, the small sins and infidelities, the very fact that your life is so ordinary and unheroic in days when the world cries out for the redemptive work of heroes: all these things can gradually become the material of the death that leads to life, if only you have eyes to see.

The Pain of Christ and the Sorrow of God

All these things can show you, over and over again, till the lesson sinks deep into your heart, the meaning of the words of our Lord: "Without me you can do nothing" (John 15:5, DR).

And so, once again, be comforted; for if you thus turn each cross as it comes into an act of love, a sacrifice, it will become a thing of light and, in the end, of joy. It is thus, and not by degrading them into a sentimentalism or an escape from reality, that we are to understand the words of our Lord: "Come unto me, all ye that labour and are heavy laden, and I will give you rest" (Matt. 11:28, KJV).

Let us return, then, to the questions with which we began. Could you keep your faith in God intact in the miseries and horrors of a concentration camp? The answer must surely be that if you had been thus prepared, you would be more likely to go on undismayed. You would put this agony, too, into the hands of God, and you would know that there, whatever might happen, it would be safe.

And is it right to be happy in your faith in God's love while the world about you is drenched in suffering? Again, the answer must surely be that it is right to be happy as the saints are happy — the light of life and love shining in their eyes even while their bodies are tortured or their minds overwhelmed by the sin and sorrow of the world. It must be right to be happy as they are happy, their faith and their love having shown them the clue to the problem of pain, having shown them how this, too, is not incompatible with divine love and divine pity but, on the contrary, is a necessary element in the whole love story: an evil out of which, in the end, love and joy are born.

But that sort of faith, that sort of happiness, is the very opposite of a self-centered contentment that takes no thought for the rest of the world. It is a faith that *shares in* all the sorrow of the world precisely because it is a faith in Christ, who took that sorrow upon Himself. We have been thinking of the fact that to be a Christian means longing to share in Christ's redemptive activity for the world; we have been thinking of vision and prayer as the essential condition of any such activity for the world; now we have the third essential element, the other essential condition of truly redemptive activity: the journey through the dark valley into the light, the journey through sorrow and death into the life of Christ.

Let us learn of human love a parable. You know how often it is through some catastrophe overcome, some deep distress or misunderstanding or infidelity surmounted, that there comes a new depth of understanding, a new depth of love, a new—a really, essentially new—life. Perhaps you say to yourself then, "I realize now that hitherto I have been simply loving myself, not really loving at all." And then, if that realization leads to the birth of real love, then what a freedom of the spirit, and what a power to help, is born in you. So it is here. Free, untrammeled, unworried, but wholly given to Love, at least trying at each moment to choose the death that leads to life instead of the pseudo-life that leads to death, you are filled with the power of the Spirit:

you know, or begin to know, in yourself the freedom of the sons of God. You become, or begin to become, in truth an *organum pulsatum a Spiritu Sancto*, an apt instrument for the Spirit's life-giving work. You become, or begin to become, one of those in whom the world's darkness is turned, through Christ's power, into light. And having day by day done your best to share with Christ in His *lama sabachthani* because, in your small way, you have turned your crosses and derelictions into the stuff of love and sacrifice, you will live always and work always in the hand of God. And at the end, not you but Christ living in you will be able to cry once again the cry of glory and achievement: *Consummatum est.*

6

Between Two Thieves

And one of the robbers who were hanged
blasphemed him.... But the other ...
said to Jesus: Lord, remember me when
thou shalt come into thy kingdom.

—Luke 23:39–42, DR

Christ was crucified between two thieves. From each of them, let us learn a final lesson. There was one who blasphemed Christ: it is a warning to us that, even though one is very near to Him — as we who, through His mercy, have been brought to know Him and be constantly near Him in His Church — still one may fail to see and to understand; still, at the end, one may be lost. Once before, He had said, "Power has gone out from me" (Luke 8:46, Knox) — power to quicken and heal — and you would have thought that here, above all, as He hung on the Cross, that power would be mighty to heal and renew the soul of a man. Yet the robber blasphemed him; and it reminds us that there can be a state of soul against which Love itself is powerless because it has hardened itself against Love.

Hell is essentially a state of being that we fashion for ourselves: a state of final separateness from God that is the result not of God's repudiation of man but of man's repudiation of God, and a repudiation that is eternal precisely because it has become, in itself, immovable. There are analogies in human experience: the hate that is so blind, so dark, that love only makes it the more violent; the pride that is so stony that humility only makes it the more scornful; the inertia — last, but not least, the inertia — that has so taken possession of the personality that no crisis, no appeal, no inducement whatsoever, can stir it into activity but, on the contrary, makes it bury itself the more deeply in its immobility. So with the soul and God: pride can become hardened into Hell, hatred can become hardened into Hell, any of the seven root forms of wrongdoing can harden into Hell, and not least that sloth that is boredom with divine things, the inertia that cannot be troubled to repent, even though it sees the abyss into which the soul is falling, because for so long, in little ways perhaps, it has accustomed itself to refuse whatever might cost it an effort. May God in His mercy save us from that.

But there is the other robber; and from the glory revealed in this apparently unlikely material, there is much that we can learn.

And first the lesson of great comfort. You remember our Lord's words to St. Peter about the forgiveness of sin: "Not seven times, but seventy times seven times" (see Matt. 18:22). It is never too late. You remember the man who had been on his back for thirty-eight years and then, in the end, received the healing touch of Christ (John 5:2ff.). It is never too late. And if we have to look back on a long series of failures, if it seems, looking back, that all the attempts we have made to serve God fully have always dwindled away into nothing almost as soon as they were begun, still it is never too late to start again. We never exhaust the infinity of the patience of Love.

But this is a case unparalleled in the life of our Lord. He does not just tell the thief that he shall have the Kingdom. "*This day* shalt thou be with me in paradise" (Luke 23:43, DR). Do you think of this as some special, and specially dramatic, form of God's mercy: so near the end of His own agony, He ignores the claims of divine justice, He wipes away with a word the evildoing of years, and makes a gift of unique prodigality, quite outside the ordinary economy of providence? No, Heaven, too, is essentially a state of being, a state of perfect oneness with God, no more arbitrary than Hell. If the robber is to be at once with Christ in Paradise, it is because he will be immediately ready; he will have achieved the perfection of love. It will be because God will say of him what He said of Magdalen: Many sins are forgiven him, are turned into glory, because he has loved much (see Luke 7:47).

Let us note immediately how much that fact, too, is a comfort and an encouragement for us, so conscious of the burden of sin that weighs us down. At the end, it is said, we shall be judged on love. You cannot, of course, say, "Then I need not bother about sins: it will be all right as long as I love God." Our Lord told us: "If you love me, keep my commandments" (John 14:15, DR). The more you love God, the harder you will try not to sin. If you try not at all, it means that you love not at all. But the trying is all. We are never to be depressed and hopeless about past failures;

we are meant to make them the material of a deeper love. We are never to worry in a self-centered way about our sinfulness; we are to keep our eyes on the Lord, trying to love Him better. Christianity is not a negative thing, not just the avoidance of things that are wrong. Christianity is love; and love, if it is deep enough and strong enough, will always cover a multitude of sins.

But the startling thing in the story of the thief remains unexplained. This change of heart, this flooding in of the love that makes Heaven, is as instantaneous, apparently, as the effect of our Lord's physical touch on the bodies of men. And how could that be? Such sudden changes do indeed take place, from dark to light, from hatred to love, provided that the soul is not set in the final hardening of Hell. But what causes them? You can think here of a tone of voice, a look from the eyes of Christ: but these things are what they are because they express the personality behind them, express, in this case, the blinding beauty of uncreated Love. The thief sees in a flash of revelation what our Lord *is*. Not of the eyes, the lips, the hands, in themselves, but of the personality it was that said, "Power has gone out from me."

And here there is a double lesson for us. First, for us, too, the way to life, the way to receive the healing power of Christ, is to forget ourselves and look at Him. *Oculi mei semper ad Dominum*, "my eyes always on the Lord": absorbed not in self-analysis and self-culture but in adoration. Only to the adoring soul are revealed the truth and beauty that beget love.

But secondly, of us, too, it is true, for better or for worse, that we affect others in the last resort by what we are. From us, too, power will go forth in our small measure, to heal or to hurt, in accordance with our state of being. Too easily we forget this central fact of human life: that always and inevitably we are affecting other people. We think too exclusively in material terms; we forget the power of spirit. We think too exclusively in terms of outward activity; we forget the power of being. If we are filled with egoism, hatred, the dark forces of life, then we spread darkness and bitterness about us whatever we may do or say. If we are filled with love, then it is light and joy that go forth from us and affect the world even though we may be remote from human contact. We know what it means to be lapped in the love of another human being, to be energized by it, healed, strengthened, renewed. We have to see that that is true of the whole world, the battleground of these opposing forces: partly a haunted house where evil that was done long ago lingers and is active, partly holy ground where the influence of love lingers on, to the healing of humanity. We have to think of the simple saints, the hermits in their cells, and see them for what they really are: playing a major part in the world's destiny, in the shaping of the world's future, simply because they are love-filled and love goes forth from them. To spread that kind of influence is the first duty of the Christian to the world in which he lives.

The Pain of Christ and the Sorrow of God

But the mark of the love that comes from God is that it is universal; it makes no discriminations. This man who, out of all the race of men, was taken with Christ to Paradise, was a robber, an outcast from society. And so he reminds us of the special duty of the Christian towards the outcasts, the fact that they in particular have a claim on our love. They may be outcasts because they have flouted a conventional code; they may be outcasts in the eyes of a class prejudice — whenever such prejudice is in question, the very antithesis of Christian brotherhood, we should think of the *Agape*, the love feast, of the primitive Christians; they may be outcasts because they have fallen from moral rectitude: it makes no matter. Our Lord ate with publicans and sinners. These poor children of God have a special claim on Christian love because they have special need of it. "The poor, the needy, you have always with you" (see John 12:8), always challenging the reality of your love of God. "I was hungry and you gave me not to eat; I was thirsty and you gave me not to drink" (Matt. 25:42). You remember the indignant astonishment of the people in our Lord's story: "Lord, when did we see you hungry …?" And then His answer: "Inasmuch as you did not do it to these my little ones you did not do it unto me" (see Matt. 25:44, 45). Remember, too, the innumerable tales of the saints who saw Christ in the beggar asking for alms: they were seeing not the nonessentials, as we in our pride and blindness so often do, but the essentials, the image and likeness of God.

On the other hand, see the further thing that this story can reveal to us. Suppose that you do see Christ in the outcast who comes to you. Suppose that you do give him food for his hunger and a fire to warm him and a place to rest his tired bones, and that you do all this with *love*, the love that warms not the body merely but the heart. Then your actions will, for him, be echoing the words of Christ to the robber: this day you may be making for him a paradise at least on earth; and you may also be the human instrument through whom God will reveal love to him and so lead him to that other, eternal Paradise, in which there are no outcasts anymore forever.

Let us return for a moment to the ideas we were thinking over earlier. We are to try to be in the company not of the betrayers but of the betrayed; trying to live for Christ and in Christ, in loving obedience to His will. We are to share the silence and stillness of soul of Mary: the life of prayer that means vision, that means living in eternity here and now. We are to make that dark journey that leads to the death of the false self in order that the true life may be born in us, so that then, putting all things into the hands of God, we may be truly ourselves because truly His. And all these things are different aspects of a single thing, different aspects of love: the love that makes the center of life not the self but the Other, and therefore turns the self into a glad instrument of the Other's will and work. Christianity bids us climb, in God's power, the ladder that leads to God, but always there is that other ladder, descending from

Heaven, bringing back to earth, bringing back to all men and especially to the needy and the outcast, the healing power of God. Contemplation thus inevitably overflows into action; and the action is a divine healing through divine power. "To me, to live is Christ," St. Paul tells us (Phil. 1:21, DR): to live is Christ, and to act is to act in the power of Christ. So, in the same activity, we love and serve both God and man.

There is one simple way in which we can try to make sure that our activity is indeed Christ acting through us. You remember Christ's last words of all: "Father, into thy hands I commend my spirit" (Luke 23:46, DR). If, before starting any work for men, any speaking or writing or activity that will directly affect men, any puzzling over a problem that concerns others as well as yourself, you make a habit of invoking the holy Spirit, the Bringer of Wisdom, and then say with Christ the words of Christ, "Into thy hands ...," then you are doing your best to put the thing into God's hands, to make it part of his will and his wisdom, and so you can cease to worry about the result because you can leave the result to Him.

And if that giving of yourself and your activity into His hands is complete, and completely trusting, then indeed you cannot know how often God may be using you in order to say through you to one or another of His children, "This day thou shalt be with me in paradise." You cannot know the extent to which you will have shared, in the end, in His saying of the same words to the whole Church, which is His Bride.

But you yourself, when the end comes for you, you will have taught yourself to say *In manus tuas*, as He did: not simply of isolated actions in your daily life, but of your life as a whole. It will then be the whole of your life that you will lay, as He did, in God's hands. And so in you, as in the penitent thief, He will see the glory of the love that covers a multitude of sins. And so He will take your life from you, as He did from the thief, a gift from your hands, and you, in your turn, will hear the words that wipe away forever the tears from the eyes of man: "Amen, I say to thee, this day thou shalt be with me in paradise."

7

THE SORROW OF GOD

You may remember a scene toward the end of Helen
Waddell's *Peter Abelard* in which Peter and Thibault
hear a terrible cry in the woods like the scream of a child
in agony, and they find a rabbit caught in a trap; they free
it, and it nuzzles into Peter's arms and dies.

It was that last confiding thrust that broke Abelard's
heart....

"Thibault," he said, "do you think there is a God
at all? Whatever has come to me, I earned it. But
what did this one do?"

Thibault nodded.

"I know," he said. "Only—I think God is in it too."

Abelard looked up sharply.

"In it? Do you mean that it makes Him suffer the
way it does us?"

"All this," he stroked the limp body, "is because
of us. But all the time God suffers. More than we do."

Abelard looked at him, perplexed....

"Thibault, do you mean Calvary?"

Thibault shook his head. "That was only a piece of
it—the piece that we saw—in time. Like that." He

pointed to a fallen tree beside them, sawn through the middle. "That dark ring there, it goes up and down the whole length of the tree. But you only see it where it is cut across. That is what Christ's life was; the bit of God that we saw. And we think God is like that, because Christ was like that, kind, and forgiving sins, and healing people. We think God is like that for ever, because it happened once, with Christ. But not the pain. Not the agony at the last. We think that stopped."

Abelard looked at him....

"Then, Thibault," he said slowly, "you think that all this ... all the pain of the world, was Christ's cross?"

"God's cross," said Thibault. "And it goes on."

"The Patripassian heresy," muttered Abelard mechanically. "But, oh God, if it were true. Thibault, it must be. At least, there is something at the back of it that is true. And if we could find it—it would bring back the whole world."[5]

Now Thibault the good and simple is here, I think, voicing a conviction common to those who have learned to know God through prayer and goodness of heart. We could state that conviction thus:

We know that love cannot but be involved in the suffering of what it loves.

[5] Helen Waddell, *Peter Abelard: A Novel* (New York: Henry Holt, 1947), 262–264.

But God is love; therefore, God cannot but be involved in the suffering of what He loves.

But He loves all His creatures; therefore, He cannot but be involved in the sufferings of all His creatures.

Against this conviction Abelard voices the doubts of the theologian. Let me say at once: I have been told that this novel is bad history; certainly Abelard is here guilty at one point of very poor theology. We need only mention Patripassianism in order to set it aside. The belief that the Father must have suffered as well as the Son followed from the belief of the Sabellians that all three Persons of the Trinity must have been incarnate. Thibault's remark about God's cross should provoke no such comment. The Incarnation means the union of two natures, divine and human, in one person, the Divine Person of the Word; and it follows from that that the actions and experiences we attribute to Christ we can attribute also to God. Christ suffered, Christ bore the Cross to Calvary, Christ died. But Christ is God, and so we rightly say God suffered, God bore His Cross to Calvary, God died. Christ's Cross is indeed God's Cross.

But there is nonetheless a real and evident difficulty. It is all very well to *say* that God suffered and so on; but what can the words really mean? God is either infinite and perfect, or He is not God. But to be infinite and perfect means to be outside the possibility of change and imperfection; in other words, to be impassible. Are we really playing with words when we say God suffered?

The Pain of Christ and the Sorrow of God

The answer is emphatically no. We could say, God became man precisely in order to suffer. How can sin be called a *felix culpa*, a blessed thing? Because it is part—a necessary part—of Love's full self-revelation. You have to think of the whole story of creation, Fall, and Redemption as the choosing by God of an order of things in which the fullness of love would be revealed in a way far beyond the possibilities of a sinless world.

Suppose the Incarnation without the Fall: we would have known much of the love and the condescension of God, but we would not have known their fullness. We would, as Tyrrell put it, have known Christ, but not Jesus; the King, but not the Savior. We would not have known that penultimate glory of love that we call *compassion*. All creation is an expression of the beauty and the love of God. Suppose many worlds of creatures, in the manner of Mr. C.S. Lewis; suppose that on earth alone sin has abounded; then on earth also grace has most abounded. The self-revelation of God through His creation has reached its furthest point. Human love itself can make the point very clear to us: it has its idyllic honeymoon stage—its "state of innocence"—when no shadow has yet fallen; but it is after the shadows have come, the crosses and perplexities and perhaps divisions, that its fullness is called forth, and that the deep wisdom and understanding, the deep peace, the deep compassion, are achieved. We know that God is involved in the suffering of His creation. He became man in order to be so involved, in order to show us these things.

But again, another difficulty arises. People say, "Yes, but all this, wonderful as it is, is in the past. Christ suffered once, at a given moment in history, but now He is glorified; He is impassible; it is all over. But the pain of the world goes on. The pain of the world goes on, but Christ is in glory. It is as though, after the brief moment of sharing with us, the veil of impassibility had descended again, and even Christ the Savior is remote from us. How can He be involved, in any sense that matters, in the agonies of the world *today*?"

This is a difficulty that many people feel; but it is, in reality, a misunderstanding. It is a misunderstanding, in the first place, of the meaning of the Cross. The simple Act of Contrition that we learned as children preparing for Confession bids us tell God we are sorry for our sins "because they have crucified my loving Savior Jesus Christ." Christ did not die merely for the sins that were then being committed or had been committed in the past: it was the total evil of the world, past, present and future, that was responsible for Calvary. And as with the sin, so with the suffering that is the effect of sin: wherever you find it, there is the Cross, sharing it in order to redeem it, to bring good out of it.

People say, "Oh, but you can't hurt God." This is the first way in which they are wrong. When I sin now, I as surely crucify God as did the soldiers on the hill of Golgotha. And similarly, when I suffer now, God is as surely involved in that suffering as He was in the sorrows of the city over which He wept (see Luke 19:41–44). We live in a time world, and so we tend to be tyrannized over by time, to lose sight of the wider horizons. And yet time is so very unimportant. We say, "This suffering is made so much lighter for me because So-and-so is sharing it with me," but is the simultaneity in time of such importance? Would it make any difference if he had taken his share in advance? The essentials are the knowledge, the involvement, the sharing: that is all. And on the Cross, Christ had knowledge of every suffering that was to come after and was involved in it, since He was suffering in order to heal or transform it and so was sharing in it and offering it to his Father, together with His own suffering, for the renewal of the world. The Crucifixion was an event in time; but the Cross transcends time.

But this putting of God's sorrow into the past is a misunderstanding for another reason. When we say that God became man in order to suffer with and for His creatures, we must not fall into a sort of practical (or imaginative) Arianism. We must not think that God, in order to be somehow involved, created a Christ to suffer while the Godhead itself remained immune, unperturbed in its immutable beatitude. God suffered. That does not mean that the divine nature underwent a diminution and became subject to evil. But it does mean that *in* the divine nature there is a quality, to speak *humano modo*, of which the human quality of pity and compassion is the expression and, so to say, the evocation. God is love, and therefore, to say that love, given the fact of misery, implies pity is to say that God, given the fact of misery, implies pity. When I share in the suffering of someone I love, that actual sharing is the expression of something deeper, something permanent: the will to share, which is what we call love. And so in the mystery of redemption: the actual sharing is done through the humanity of Christ, but that actual sharing is the expression of the deeper and permanent mystery in the Godhead, the will to share — i.e., the will to be a *companion*.

That permanence — and, in God, it is the permanence, the immutability, of eternity — is what Thibault expressed in his image of the tree trunk. The Cross is the bit of God that we see, because it is God acting visibly, through a human body and soul. But as God acts, so He is; and what He is, He is eternally and unchangeably. Here again we are misled by our categories of time. We tend to think, "What is the good of having compassion for what is past, since if it is past, you cannot affect it; or for what is future, since by the time it comes to be, you and your sympathy may have ceased to be?" And similarly we tend to think, "God's will to share decreed the Cross, yes; and therefore at that historical moment of time, the will to share was operative, effective; but it could not affect the sufferings of the past, since they were then over; it could not affect the sufferings of the future, since, by the time they occurred, the Cross itself had given way to the Resurrection and the glory." We forget that because we, for our part, live in a world of events, of coming to be and passing away, we think of all reality in terms of the successiveness of our own experience. The events that are so real today will soon be lost in the mists of history. But in the life of God, there are no events; God has no history. Eternity is not an endless line running parallel with the line of time; it is a point; and what to us is past or future is as much present to eternity as is the actual moment we are now living.

John of St. Thomas uses the figure of a tree so large as to stretch over all the waters of a river, thus coexisting with all the parts of the river together even though these succeed one another. Or again, you can imagine the sequence of created events as a sort of Bayeux tapestry, and we who are in time as walking along close beside it, so that only the event immediately before us is present to us and the rest is either remembered in the past or unknown in the future; but the gaze of eternity is, on the contrary, like a spectator so distant but with sight so keen as to be able to see the whole tapestry at once, as a whole.

This is indeed the force of the famous definition of Boethius, which St. Thomas adopted and which makes clear the difference between eternity and perpetuity. Eternity, writes Boethius "is the perfect possession altogether of an endless life"; and he goes on to explain how, since it "comprehends and possesses the whole plenitude of endless life together, so that no future part is lacking to it, nor anything that is past has flowed away from it, it follows that such a life is rightly called eternal, having itself always present to itself, and at the same time having an infinity of moving time equally present to it."[6] And so Boethius goes on to speak of the knowledge of God: for, he says, if you wish to estimate that *praesentia*

---

[6] Boethius, *The Consolation of Philosophy* 5, 6.

whereby God discerns all things, you will more rightly think of it as the knowledge of a never-fading instant than as a foreknowledge as of things to come. For which reason we speak not of God's *praevidentia* but of his *providentia*, because, placed far above inferior things, he overlooks all things, as it were, from the highest summit of things.

Thus, the very immutability of God is not a denial of His involvement in the sorrows of these present times, but a triumphant vindication of it. Of the human body of Christ you can say that first it suffered and then it was glorified and made glad; but throughout that temporal sequence, the Godhead remains unchanged, and unchanged precisely in its knowledge and willing of, and its will to share in, that which Christ on the Cross took to Himself and made His own and in His glorification turned into glory.

That last phrase can lead us on to the solution of what may perhaps be a last remaining difficulty. The conclusion so far is this: that the mystery of divine pity is expressed temporally in the Passion of Christ, but that in and behind that temporal event there lies the eternity of the will to share; so that, even if you were to say, incorrectly, that the Passion is "all over and done with," still you would have to say that the divine involvement in the pain of creatures is an ever-present reality. But is there not an ambiguity about the expression "will to share"? For if we safeguard the perfection of God's beatitude, shall we not be emptying the phrase of its power to satisfy our hearts? And if, on the other hand, we give it the fullness of meaning our hearts demand, shall we not be doing violence to the nature of God?

The Pain of Christ and the Sorrow of God

Let us put it as plainly as possible. To feel compassion means that when the rabbit is hurt, you are hurt too; when the rabbit feels pain, you feel pain too. And if, foreknowing the future, you have the will to share in the pain that you know is to come, then that will is itself already in some sort a pain. As the anticipation of joy is itself a joy (and often, poor things that we are, a greater joy than the actuality will be), so the anticipation of sorrow is itself a sorrow. But in the Godhead there cannot be pain. Can the will to share, therefore, be anything more than a remote unruffled benevolence? Yes, it can, and I think we shall see how if we try to plumb the reality of love and the meaning of God's providence a little deeper.

After the Cross, the Resurrection; after the Passion, the apotheosis; but in God there is no *after*. Just as, in the depths of the Godhead, there is the mystery that is the identity of justice and mercy, so, in the depths of the Godhead, is there not likewise a mystery in which compassion and triumph are one? Indeed, even in human love, is there not some far-off suggestion of this? Is it not possible to know an agony of compassion that at the same time is deep joy? The same thing can cause sorrow for the suffering that it is and joy for the enrichment and deepening of being that it brings about.

And that surely, in passing, is just what Purgatory is; and it explains why St. Bede the Venerable can speak of Purgatory as a flowered meadow, so lovely that the observer mistook it for Heaven. And when the soul enters into its glory, the joy is fulfilled, but the sorrow is not forgotten, is not as though it had never been; on the contrary, it is surely part of the very stuff of the glory. If Virgil and Dante were right when they said that there is no misery like the remembrance of having once been happy, then perhaps the converse is equally true: that there is no happiness like the memory of having been sad, provided at least that the sorrow is the material out of which the happiness is forged. So our Lord speaks of the sorrow of the woman in labor being turned into joy when the child is born into the world (see John 16:21)—not simply a temporal sequence of unrelated states, but a turning, a transforming of the one thing into the other. But in God there is no *after*.

And if you could, so to say, telescope these temporal successions into the unity of a *nunc stans*, what would you have? You would have something transcending both of the terms our successive experience separates. You would have something of which there is perhaps a hint in the moment at which the penitent receives the grace of sacramental forgiveness, and is bowed in sorrow and at the same time, and *in* that very sorrow, finds the joy of reunion with God—a joy, that is to say, that cannot be known apart from the sorrow because the sorrow is in some mysterious way a component part of it, or rather, the material of it. And so again, as the deepest tragedy is said to be that in which there is an element of laughter, so the deepest joy is that in which there is the trace of tears.

These are human things; it would be folly to predicate them immediately of God. But they point us, I think, in the right direction. And we shall go further if we examine the notion of sacrifice.

The Pain of Christ and the Sorrow of God

Canon Masure, in *The Christian Sacrifice*, has some very il-
luminating lines in this connection. He has been speaking of
the two elements in sacrifice, the oblation with immolation,
and the apotheosis or communion with the deity; and he
points out how the fact that the offering and renunciation
of a secondary good is costly or painful is due to sin. Were
there no sin in the world, there would still be the duty of
sacrifice; but the word *sacrifice* would not have the painful
connotations that it has for us today. We have a clue to
this in ordinary human experience. If I am asked to give up
to a stranger something I value very much, I do it, if at all,
only at cost of much inner struggle; but to give the same
thing to someone I love is no struggle at all: I am happy to
give it, and should be less happy if I valued it less. In the
case of the stranger, happiness may come afterward; I may
be happy because I have done the thing; but at best, there
are two successive stages. But in the second case there is
no time lag; there is no distinction: the giving is itself the
happiness. So it would be with sacrifice to God in a sinless
world; and so Canon Masure writes:

> Let us suppose (a vanished dream) that we could join
> together *in momento, in ictu oculi*, the struggle and its
> issue, means and end; the grief, which is the tension
> between that which is and that which ought to be,
> would exist no longer. Today, when we have brought
> some undertaking to successful issue, we try to forget

the labour which it has cost us, like the mother in the Gospel, and sometimes we achieve it; we are even happy to have suffered! But we can imagine a state in which we should be happy to suffer, or rather simply to act, because the action, telescoped with its result, would not have been suffering at all.

And he points out how the saints, who are "almost at the term of their supernatural development," seem to have reached the stage at which "grief has changed its meaning and become joy"; so our Lord speaks of his joy at the approaching Passion—and it is only comparatively recently in the Church's history that the representation of Christ reigning and triumphant upon the Cross gives way to the exclusive portrayal of human suffering and tragedy—and His disciples follow Him here as elsewhere, and are at their gayest when they go to meet their deaths.

We are here at the very heart of Christian optimism. It blinds its eyes to no single crime or wickedness; there is no cry from humanity or from the lesser creatures to which it is deaf; it knows the problem of evil in all its terrible fullness; and yet nonetheless it affirms at the end with Julian of Norwich, "All shall be well, and all manner of things shall be well." In other words, it has faith in what, to the eyes of eternity, is already and always an accomplished vision: the fulfilment of sorrow *in joy.*

The same Julian of Norwich has another analogy that may help us, when she speaks of the love-longing of Christ for His brethren; and the student of theology might say, "But how can there be longing, desire, still in Christ, since He is glorified and in the state of beatitude wherein all desires are fulfilled?" But the answer is, I think, that Christ longs for the presence with Him of His Body, which is the Church, in the same way that, according to St. Thomas, the soul in glory longs for the resurrection of the flesh: a longing, a desire, that is not incompatible with perfect beatitude because it is welcomed as part of the total love story, and because — unlike our human desires on earth — it has in it the certainty of fulfillment.

And finally, the same is true when we think of the blessed in Heaven in relation to those they love on earth. When Dante on earth sinned or was unhappy, did it leave Beatrice in Heaven unconcerned? On the contrary, the involvement is greater to the extent to which the vision of the blessed is greater and deeper than was their awareness on earth. When Dante sinned, then, did Beatrice suffer? We cannot say yes without qualification, for that would deny her beatitude. But neither can we say no without qualification, for that would be to deny her love. We can only say that she had compassion — i.e., that she suffered with Dante, in the way proper to the blessed, the way proper to those who have telescoped means and end, who see the issue in the struggle, who see the good, which is love, emerging from evil and the evil only in terms of that triumphant good. For that involvement we have no words, for our human experience cannot know it; but at least we can see it as a transcending of joy and sorrow, a transcending of both, which destroys the love-reality of neither.

And so we can return to Abelard and Thibault and the rabbit. "'God's cross,' said Thibault. 'And it goes on.'" What *ought* Abelard to have answered? If these thoughts have not led us astray, we can say that he ought to have answered: "Yes, Thibault, you are right. It goes on, first because, though the Crucifixion was an event in time, it was God who was crucified; and to the theandric involvement that the Crucifixion expressed and effected, all temporal events, past, present and future, were all equally present. It goes on, secondly, because, while the mystery of divine pity is temporally expressed in Calvary through the humanity of Christ, it is also eternally and constantly present in the depths of the Godhead, not indeed in the form of suffering as humanity knows it, but as the eternal will to share that is thus revealed as an aspect of infinite love—a will to share that is no fiction or play upon words but the true involvement of a state of being in which the imperfections of joy and sorrow as we know them are transcended in the fullness of creative and redeeming love."

But now, there is something else that Abelard might have said; and it will lead us on to consider finally the practical implications of these ideas. Abelard might have said, "Yet, it goes on, for though the Cross, as a physical event in time, is past and over, it goes on day by day in the sacrifice of the Mass."

It was necessary that Christ should suffer and so enter into His glory (see Luke 24:26). There you have the two moments of all sacrifice: the immolation, the apotheosis. The victim is offered and given, and accepted by God; and then, the victim being as it were divinized by that acceptance, the offerer is divinized or glorified in his turn through communion with the victim. Those two moments—and we must never separate them in our thought—are, of course, found once again in the Mass: one and the same sacrifice as that of the Cross, differing only in the mode of its offering. The Mass is not just a memorial of Calvary; not a repetition of Calvary; but the same essential act. The physical pain and the mental dereliction: these are over; but the Cross was the expression, through the humanity, of the eternal will to share; and the Mass is the same essential expression of the same will to share. God's Cross goes on. Not a sparrow falls to the ground, today as yesterday, but our heavenly Father has care of it (Matt. 10:29). And through the humanity of the Son, it is a *redeeming* care.

But, as the Pope had made very clear to us, in this redemptive process that goes on day by day, the Head of the Mystical Body needs the members, needs the prayer and penance of the faithful. By sharing in the Mass, we share in the Cross and the fruits of the Cross. But how do we share in the Mass?

The Mass is first an offering. It is the self-offering of Christ, but of Christ the Head; and it is therefore the offering of the *totus Christus*, Christ together with the members of His Body. "Brethren, pray that my sacrifice and yours …": we are meant to share in the sacrifice by offering ourselves and our whole lives, our world, the lesser creation over which man is meant to have dominion, in and through the offering of Christ. Insofar as we offer fully, immolate fully, we shall find full redemption. For us, too, apotheosis will follow. And insofar as we offer fully and immolate fully, we shall share in the divine compassion and its healing effect. But what is the immolation we have to carry out?

Immolation is renunciation, and, in the last resort, renunciation of the self. To use an awkward but traditional word, it is detachment. But what is the condition of all true detachment, the ability to care and not care, the ability to leave everything gladly or at least willingly in the hands of God? The condition is to free ourselves as far as possible from the tyranny of time. For us on earth, there is no *tota simul et perfecta possessio* but only the fleeting moment. And hardly has beauty come to be but it is passing away, and joy eludes us like the running waters of a stream. And so we cling and clutch and try impotently to make the temporal present an eternal now. We cannot renounce; we merely lose. Louis MacNeice writes in one of his poems:

> Do not then turn maudlin or weathercock,
> We must cut the throat of the hour
> That it may not haunt us because our sentiments
> Continued its existence to pollute
> Its essence: bottled time turns sour on the sill.

And so Bl. Henry Suso tells us: "Be steadfast, and never rest content until thou hast obtained the now of eternity as thy present possession in this life, so far as this is possible to human infirmity." And how is this to be done? By seeing all things and events in God, and God in all things and events, and therefore taking them all from His hands. Suso tells us again:

> The minds and thoughts of these men have so passed away into God, and they know nothing, as it were, of themselves, save only that they view themselves and all things in their primal fountain-head; and therefore they have the same pleasure and complacency in each several thing which God does ... and thus it is that their will is absolute in might, for heaven and earth serve them, and every creature is subject to them.... Such persons feel no sorrow of heart about anything—you will notice this echo of what we were thinking just now—for I only call that pain and sorrow of heart which the will with full deliberation wishes to be freed from. Externally indeed they have a sense of pleasure and pain like other people, and it is more intense in them perhaps than others, because of their great tenderness; but in their inmost souls it finds no abiding-place, and exteriorly they remain firm against impatience. They are filled to the full, even in this life, so far as this is possible, owing to their detachment from self, and so their joy is complete and stable in all things.

"Cast your cares upon the Lord," we are told (see 1 Pet. 5:7, DR). If we can find in the Mass, as we should, the power to put ourselves and all things unreservedly into God's hands and to live in the present, we shall be sharing fully in the self-offering of Christ, and we shall at the same time be coming to the understanding of that paradox that the lives of the saints reveal: the paradox of utter caring and utter not caring, of supreme sorrow and supreme joy. We shall be sharing in the sorrow and the joy of Christ.

But—this is the final point—it will not be just a joy springing from the wisdom that can accept all things because it sees how love rules and embraces all things: it will be a redemptive joy. Not the *stasis* of ultimate beatitude, but the *dynamis* of redemption. The sacrifice offering, the renunciation of self, is itself what brings about the apotheosis, the healing for ourselves and for the world. Out of the sorrow comes the joy; out of the Cross the Resurrection; out of the immolation the communion; and the communion in the Mass is not merely an individual but also a cosmic thing. "We thinke," wrote Donne,

> that *Paradise* and *Calvarie*,
> *Christs* Crosse and *Adams* tree, stood in one place;
> Looke Lord, and finde both *Adams* met in me;
> As the first *Adams* sweat surrounds my face,
> May the last *Adams* blood my soule embrace.[7]

We have lost something, in more recent centuries, of the perfect balance that characterizes here the primitive Church: we have lost the sense of triumph in the Cross. The memory of the Passion on Fridays, the days of penance, is no longer linked in our minds with the memory of the Resurrection on Sundays, and the festival day of rest

[7] John Donne, "Hymn to God, My God, in My Sickness."

and rejoicing becomes all too often a Sahara of sabbatarian gloom. And so we have lost our sense of balance about suffering in general: we isolate it, we of little faith, from apotheosis, as, in the later Middle Ages, they isolated the human suffering of the Passion from the joy and the triumph. And so we can only wring our hands in impotence when the rabbit screams.

But God's Cross goes on; and slowly, constantly thwarted by our perversity and blindness and evil but still continuing, the revelation of love's meaning goes on. Evil produces its ineluctable consequences, and the world is drenched in pain; but at every point in time and space where pain has its kingdom, there also are the tears of God, and sooner or later, through the tears, the soul of the world is renewed.

About the Author

Born in England in 1906, Gerald Vann entered the Dominican Order in 1923 and, after completing his theological studies in Rome, was ordained a priest in 1929. On returning to England, he studied modern philosophy at Oxford and was then sent to Blackfriars School in Northhamptonshire to teach and later to serve as headmaster of the school and superior of the community there. Tireless in his efforts to bolster the foundations of peace, he organized the international Union of Prayer for Peace during his tenure at Blackfriars.

Fr. Vann devoted his later years to writing, lecturing, and giving retreats in England and in the United States, including giving lectures at the Catholic University of America in Washington, D.C.

He wrote numerous articles and books, including a biography of St. Thomas Aquinas, who influenced him greatly. Fr. Vann's writings combine the philosophy and theology of St. Thomas with the humanism emphasized in the 1920s and 1930s. His works reflect his keen understanding of man's relationship to God, his deep sensitivity to human values, and his compassionate understanding of man's problems and needs. Particularly relevant in today's divided world is his appeal for unity, charity, and brotherhood. His words reveal what it means today to fulfill the two greatest commandments: to love God and to love one's neighbor.

Sophia Institute

Sophia Institute is a nonprofit institution that seeks to nurture the spiritual, moral, and cultural life of souls and to spread the Gospel of Christ in conformity with the authentic teachings of the Roman Catholic Church.

Sophia Institute Press fulfills this mission by offering translations, reprints, and new publications that afford readers a rich source of the enduring wisdom of mankind.

Sophia Institute also operates the popular online resource CatholicExchange.com. *Catholic Exchange* provides world news from a Catholic perspective as well as daily devotionals and articles that will help readers to grow in holiness and live a life consistent with the teachings of the Church.

In 2013, Sophia Institute launched Sophia Institute for Teachers to renew and rebuild Catholic culture through service to Catholic education. With the goal of nurturing the spiritual, moral, and cultural life of souls, and an abiding respect for the role and work of teachers, we strive to provide materials and programs that are at once enlightening to the mind and ennobling to the heart; faithful and complete, as well as useful and practical.

Sophia Institute gratefully recognizes the Solidarity Association for preserving and encouraging the growth of our apostolate over the course of many years. Without their generous and timely support, this book would not be in your hands.

www.SophiaInstitute.com
www.CatholicExchange.com
www.SophiaInstituteforTeachers.org

Sophia Institute Press® is a registered trademark of Sophia Institute.
Sophia Institute is a tax-exempt institution as defined by the
Internal Revenue Code, Section 501(c)(3). Tax ID 22-2548708.